T0207706

THE NEXT STEPS

John R. Shuman

WestBow Press books may be ordered through booksellers or by contacting:

WestBow Press
A Division of Thomas Nelson & Zondervan
1663 Liberty Drive
Bloomington, IN 47403
www.westbowpress.com
844-714-3454

ISBN: 978-1-6642-5244-8 (sc)
ISBN: 978-1-6642-5245-5 (hc)
ISBN: 978-1-6642-5243-1 (e)

Library of Congress Control Number: 2021924876

Print information available on the last page.

WestBow Press rev. date: 12/27/2021

Special Thanks

1. First, and foremost, I must thank God for the inspiration, the words, and the guidance on this book.
2. My workout buddy (read the book) Mike for planting the seed that led to this book, and for believing in me, encouraging me and being the brother that I needed you to be.
3. Belinda and Carl for following the leading of the Spirit, and prayerfully listening to His voice.
4. Natalie and Tom for assisting me with this project.
5. My prayer warriors: J.J., Larry, Brian L., Brian B., Joe, Evelyn, John, Ann, Darren, and Cheryl for lifting this up (and lifting me up as well) in prayer, praising God with me throughout the whole experience.
6. Finally (but not least) My best half Stephanie, for always being there for me throughout the good times and the bad times. I love you (T.T.W.C.)

I love all of you, and praise God daily for placing you in my life.

Dedication

I am dedicating this book to all God's children, those I have met, and those I shall meet when I see my Father's face. God has blessed you; God loves you and He cares about your entire journey.

Let Us Pray:

Dear Lord, I lift up all those that pick up this book. Open their eyes to Your words, open their hearts to the message You want them to hear, and show them the wonders You have planned for them as they take their next step with You. Lord I ask that You use these words to help those that are on this journey with You, but I really hope that You can uses these words to help people start their walk with You today.

Contents

1. Preface: Life's Journey 1
2. Direction 3
3. The First Step 6
4. Do Not Turn Back 10
5. The Next Steps 16
6. Light Up 18
7. Bulk Up 22
8. Gear Up 29
9. Grow Up 37
10. Speak Up 43
11. Step Up 47
12. Listen Up 51
13. The Hike 56
14. Hills 61

15. Valleys 64
16. Meadows 67
17. Wrong Turns 69
18. Trips 72
19. Stumbles 74
20. Potholes 77
21. Traps And Snares .81
22. Enjoy Your Time 85
23. The Journey Continues 89
24. The Last Step 92
25. One final thought .95

Preface: Life's Journey

We are all on a journey, a journey called life. We start this journey the moment we are born going with the aid of our "coaches", (our parents, grandparents, aunts, and uncles- our family and friends.) But this is just the warm-up to the actual journey we are on.

Jesus says in Luke 13:33a

> *33 In any case, I must press on today and tomorrow and the next day*

We are all on this journey, and in this book, we are going to look at where we are going, how we are getting there, things to do along the way, the hazards we will face, and what our next step should be.

I am going to try to incorporate scripture into each chapter for us to focus on, ponder, learn from, or just to inspire us. I am going to try to be informative on the path we are on to lead you further along that path. And I am going to pray along the way because we are instructed in 1 Thessalonians 5:17 (NKJV) to:

> *17 pray without ceasing,*

And because prayer is a particularly important part of the journey, providing us strength, guidance, energy, and the will to face another day.

I chose the title "The Next Steps" because of the saying "The journey of a million miles begins with just one step" and that is going to be the focus of this book... the steps along the way.

Let Us Pray:

Lord God I ask now for Your direction. Direct me as I write, direct those that read this along their journey, direct those that are on the bench so that they may begin the journey of their lifetime. Lord help my words to strengthen, encourage, build up, and lead others along the course they are on. Help me to bring awareness to the stumbling blocks, and to help those trapped in the pits and snares along the way. Lord, please help me with my next step, as I try to help these readers with their next steps.

Direction

No matter what, we are all on a journey, the questions become: 1) which direction are we going in? 2) Are we going in the right direction? 3) How can we be certain we are going in the right direction? And 4) how do I turn around if I am going in the wrong direction? These are important questions to be answered so let us look at each of them.

Which direction are we going in?

There are only two different directions, the path to righteousness and the path away from righteousness. One way the Bible puts it is death and life like in Romans 6:23

> **23** *For the wages of sin is death, but the gift of God is eternal life in Christ Jesus our Lord.*

There are your two directions, away from God (sin and death) or towards God (eternal life) There are no other paths, just death and life.

Are we going in the right direction? And how can we be certain we are going in the right direction?

We know which direction we are going in at first because Romans 3:23 tells us:

> **23** *for all have sinned and fall short of the glory of God,*

Yes, we are all sinners, each and every one of us as we can see in Romans 3:10 (NKJV)

> **10** *As it is written:*
> *"There is none righteous, no, not one;*

None of us are righteous, not even one of us. So, this means, at least at the very beginning, we are all heading in the wrong direction. We are all heading down the path of destruction, we are all going towards sin and death. But we want to be heading the other way, the path of righteousness, the path of eternal life.

Which then brings us to the last question I had...

How do I turn around if I am going in the wrong direction?

Did you read what Romans 6:23 said? Let us look at it again:

> **23** *For the wages of sin is death, but the gift of God is eternal life in Christ Jesus our Lord.*

The **GIFT** of God is eternal life. The pathway to eternal life is FREELY given to us. We must receive that gift from God, and then the MOMENT we receive that gift we are heading in the right direction. We must receive that gift from God and turn around and go on our journey towards everlasting life.

It is a matter of choice, life or death, which direction do you want to be headed towards? If we continue down the path to sin, then the choice of death has already been made. Do you want to choose life? Then you need to take the first step on your journey.

Let Us Pray:

Lord God, I am thankful for Your gift, the gift of life freely given to us from You. Lord, I Praise You for this gift because there is no other way for us to head in the right direction. We cannot make it on our own because of our sin we are heading in the wrong direction, but through You we can turn ourselves around and go in the right direction towards life and away from sin and death. Thank You for this gift and all it gives us.

The First Step

Now we know which direction we want to go in, but how do we go in that direction? How do we turn ourselves around and receive that gift from God? First, we must know what that gift is. For this, we start with John 3:16-17 (NKJV):

> **16** *For God so loved the world that He gave His only begotten Son, that whoever believes in Him should not perish but have everlasting life.* **17** *For God did not send His Son into the world to condemn the world, but that the world through Him might be saved.*

The gift is Jesus, the Son of God, and to receive the gift from God we need to believe in Him. God did not send

Jesus to condemn us, for we are already condemned, we are already going in the wrong direction, God sent Jesus to us so that we are able to turn around and follow God and go toward the eternal life promised to us. Jesus even tells us this in John 10:10 (NKJV):

> **10** *The thief does not come except to steal, and to kill, and to destroy. I have come that they may have life, and that they may have it more abundantly.*

Jesus came to give us life, more life than we could have ever dreamed of. More life than we could ever hope for, eternal life with God in heaven.

But, alas, I still have not answered that important question of what the first step is. Romans 10:9 (NKJV) tells us that we must:

> **9** *that if you confess with your mouth the Lord Jesus and believe in your heart that God has raised Him from the dead, you will be saved.*

We must confess our sins and believe in our heart that Jesus is the Son of God, raised from the dead and that He conquered sin and death by being resurrected from the grave. But how do we do that? How do we confess our sins and believe in our heart? Well, the answer is this... seek, ask, and knock! Matthew 6:33 (NKJV) tells us to first:

> *33 But seek first the kingdom of God and His righteousness, and all these things shall be added to you.*

And Matthew 7:7-8 also tells us:

> *7 "Ask, and it will be given to you; seek, and you will find; knock, and it will be opened to you. 8 For everyone who asks receives, and he who seeks finds, and to him who knocks it will be opened.*

Our first step is to seek God, it does us no good if we are not seeking Him because we must first seek in order to find. If we are not seeking God, we will not find Him, and therefore we will not find his gift for us. Then we must ask, we cannot receive the gift if we do not ask for it, and the last of the first steps is to knock so the doorway can be opened, and we may enter the path to righteousness.

How do you do all of that, you ask? The answer is simple, with a prayer. One that goes something like this:

> "God, I am a sinner, and I am not worthy to come before You. But I have heard that You sent Your Son, Jesus, to be the sacrifice for my sin. You sent Your Son to die on the cross because of the sin I have committed. Please forgive me God, please forgive my sins, and allow me to enter Your kingdom. I know

> that I do not deserve this; Your Word tells me that no one is righteous and worthy, but it also says You loved me so much that You took care of it by sending Your Son, Jesus to save me. For this, I thank You, for this I am eternally grateful, and I praise You for forgiving me."

Once you have prayed this and ask for God's forgiveness, you have taken the first steps in the right direction, towards eternal life.

Let Us Pray:

God, I want to lift up all those that have said that prayer right now. I ask that You guide them on the journey of their life. Help them to seek You first in all that they do, help them to ask for Your help when times get hard, and help them to knock on Your door so that they may enter in and get peace and rest from being in Your presence.

Do Not Turn Back

One of the hardest parts of this journey is leaving our comfort zone (the life we are giving up, the one heading in the wrong direction) and heading towards the unknown. The Bible tells us all about this in the Old Testament when Moses leads the Jewish people out of Egypt.

I am not going to go into the entire story, so let me summarize the beginning. The Hebrews went to Egypt to escape a famine, and they were saved by God's plan to place a Hebrew (Joseph) in charge over all of Egypt's bounty and they stayed for over 400 years. During that time, they were made slaves. Their life became difficult, they were forced to make bricks, then when it was determined that this was not hard enough, they were forced to make bricks without using straw (a main item used in making bricks). They were whipped, beaten, tortured all because of their genealogy. Then along comes Moses. He negotiated (with God's help) the release of the Jewish people with the Pharoah. And they left Egypt. Now we are to Exodus 14, and I want to pick up the story beginning in verses 5-9:

> **5** *When the king of Egypt was told that the*
> *people had fled, Pharaoh and his officials*
> *changed their minds about them and said,*
> *"What have we done? We have let the*
> *Israelites go and have lost their services!"* **6**
> *So he had his chariot made ready and took*
> *his army with him.* **7** *He took six hundred*
> *of the best chariots, along with all the other*
> *chariots of Egypt, with officers over all of*
> *them.* **8** *The LORD hardened the heart of*
> *Pharaoh king of Egypt, so that he pursued*
> *the Israelites, who were marching out boldly.*
> **9** *The Egyptians—all Pharaoh's horses and*
> *chariots, horsemen and troops—pursued the*
> *Israelites and overtook them as they camped*
> *by the sea near Pi Hahiroth, opposite Baal*
> *Zephon.*

I bring this up to set the scenario, the people of Israel (the Hebrews) have gone on and now they are being pursued by a MASSIVE army 600 chariots, all the captains, and even the Pharoah himself is coming after them. And the people's response was this Exodus 14:10-12:

> ***10*** *As Pharaoh approached, the Israelites looked up, and there were the Egyptians, marching after them. They were terrified and cried out to the Lord.* ***11*** *They said to Moses, "Was it because there were no graves in Egypt that you brought us to the desert to die? What have you done to us by bringing us out of Egypt?* ***12*** *Didn't we say to you in Egypt, 'Leave us alone; let us serve the Egyptians'? It would have been better for us to serve the Egyptians than to die in the desert!"*

They feared what was behind them and said it would have been better for them to stay. Egypt was their "comfort zone". They were tortured, they were beaten, the sinful life was all they knew. God had promised them better, but they wanted to stay with what they knew.

This is the same concept we have the moment we turn towards God and take that first step on this journey. We look back at what we had and think that is what we know it is what we desire, it is our "comfort zone", but it is in the wrong direction. Our old life pursues us, we know how to behave there, we know the expectations it has (or the lack of expectations) it tries to pull us back in to it. But we need to move forward, to continue to head in the right direction.

And, obviously, this is not an easy task because we are heading into the unknown. God has promised us a better life, and we know that that will come, but we already know the life we had and so we would rather stay there.

Now God used this for a lesson to the children of Israel, He parted the sea, allowed them to cross over dry land to the other side, and when the Egyptians tried to do the same, they were drowned. And Exodus 14:30-31 tells us the end of this story:

> ***30*** *That day the Lord saved Israel from the hands of the Egyptians, and Israel saw the Egyptians lying dead on the shore.* **31** *And when the Israelites saw the mighty hand of the Lord displayed against the Egyptians, the people feared the Lord and put their trust in him and in Moses his servant.!"*

They were delivered out of that trouble by God, and they saw the wonderful thing that God had done for them in protecting them. So, they lived happily ever after, right?? Wrong! They continued to look backwards the entire time. Every time they came across a problem, they would say things like (Exodus 16:1-3):

> *"The whole Israelite community set out from Elim and came to the Desert of Sin, which is between Elim and Sinai, on the fifteenth day*

> *of the second month after they had come out of Egypt.* **2** *In the desert the whole community grumbled against Moses and Aaron.* **3** *The Israelites said to them, "If only we had died by the* LORD's *hand in Egypt! There we sat around pots of meat and ate all the food we wanted, but you have brought us out into this desert to starve this entire assembly to death."*

Every time they came across an issue they would complain and say it was better in the life we had (the one that led to death) than what they were heading towards (the life promised to them by God), And we seem to do the same thing, every time we hit a snag, run up against a problem, see a hazard in our way... we then want to run back the other way.

God is in control, God is bringing you to a better place (the children of Israel were going to the promised land, a land that was described as flowing with milk and honey, better known as having more than enough of everything they would ever need), God has a better plan for you than your old life does. [which is why we read Jeremiah 29:11(NKJV)]:

> **11** *For I know the thoughts that I think toward you, says the Lord, thoughts of peace and not of evil, to give you a future and a hope.*

We must continually look forward at what is to come, not look back and fall into the trap of our comfort zone. (more on the traps to come the chapters "Trips", "Stumbles", and "Potholes")

Let Us Pray:

God, I know the path ahead leads to a better life, one of peace, hope and life, not of evil and death. But the pull of my past is strong, and I know that You are stronger. Break the control of that past over me and help me to keep my eyes forward on the promises You have for me. Lord, I need to break away from my comfort zone and move on knowing that You are with me guiding me all the way.

The Next Steps

There are many steps we need to take next. We need to tear down our old barriers, we need to strengthen up our spiritual bodies, we need to gear up ourselves to prepare ourselves for the journey, we need to build up our defenses, and we need to step up to the task. We need to learn the ways of God, and how to communicate with Him. As with any trip, we must be ready for all that lies ahead. Preparation is key, and these are the steps we need to take to prepare ourselves for what is to come.

We need to build ourselves up, tear down our barriers, get buddies to help aid us along the way. We must learn to hear God's voice and to follow His instructions because He is here to help us not to discourage us. (Jeremiah 29:11):

> ***11*** *For I know the plans I have for you," declares the* Lord*, "plans to prosper you and not to harm you, plans to give you hope and a future.*

See, God tells us that He knows the plan (pathway) that He has for us. His plan is not to hurt us in any way but plans for hope, joy, gladness, a future (with Him always).

Let Us Pray:

Father, please help me prepare for what is to come, help me to grow, help me to mature, help me to learn, and help me to strengthen my life so that I am ready for all that is to come. Lord, help me to focus on the pathway You have for me so that I might prosper the way You plan for me to.

Light Up

They say Rome was not built in a day. What does that mean? It means it took time a lot of time. Rome was a great empire, but that is not how it started out. It grew over years and years of building. You are the same way, where you are now has taken time, but that is not a remarkable thing. Before now, you were building up a life of sin, you were on a pathway to destruction. And because of all the time spent building up those habits, it is going to take time to change them. And you are going to need to tear down and destroy those habits.

Ephesians 5:8 tells us that:

> ***8*** *For you were once darkness, but now you are light in the Lord. Live as children of light*

So, we need to walk out of darkness and be filled with the light of God. But it is going to take time. God's light is going to shine in you, and it will light up things that are hindering your relationship with Him. And when those things are brought to the light, they will need to be destroyed. Let us look back a couple of verses here to Ephesians 5:5-6:

> **5** *For of this you can be sure: No immoral, impure, or greedy person—such a person is an idolater—has any inheritance in the kingdom of Christ and of God.* **6** *Let no one deceive you with empty words, for because of such things God's wrath comes on those who are disobedient.*

These are the ways of darkness (sin) immorality, impurity, greed, lust, idolatry, and they have no purpose in God's kingdom, therefore they will not be allowed in. If these are the things that are controlling your life, they must be destroyed, and you must rid them from your life. These things are like a mold growing in the dark shadows of your home. While they are in the dark you do not realize they are there, and they grow and grow eventually destroying the home. The way to combat them is to first shine a light on them to know where they are. (You cannot kill off a mold if you do not know where it is or what type it is). Once you have found it then you can work on getting it out.

It is the same with your sinful past. It is a mold that is destroying you in the dark regions of your life. But now you have brought in the light of God, and it is shining in you. That light will shine on the mold within, and then you are going to need to decide if you are going to let it continue or are you going to get rid of it. (I say it this way because even I have left some things alone and seen them grow even though they were sinful and destroying me. Eventually I did work on getting rid of them, but I did not at first. And do not get me wrong, I am not perfect either, there are still things that the light is bringing to my attention today that I am working on)

Now, Ephesians 5 goes on to say this in verses 10-13:

> ***10*** *and find out what pleases the Lord.* ***11*** *Have nothing to do with the fruitless deeds of darkness, but rather expose them.* ***12*** *It is shameful even to mention what the disobedient do in secret.* ***13*** *But everything exposed by the light becomes visible—and everything that is illuminated becomes a light.*

Everything that is exposed to the light becomes visible, it cannot hide from the light. And once we have exposed it, we can deal with it.

I know old habits are hard to break, and so just as Rome was not built in a day, neither were those habits, so it is going to take some time, it is going to take some strength to stand up to them, and you may even need to get some help to overcome them. But you must tear down those walls in order to build a better life.

Let Us Pray:

God, shine Your light into my darkest corners. Expose what is trying to hide in the shadows so that I might be able to address the cause and rid the mold from my life. Shine Your light in me so that I might see what is holding me back, so I can see what is tying me down and I can then seek the help I need and thereby follow You even closer than before. Help me to seek out the mold that is trying to destroy me, so that I can rid it from my life.

Bulk Up

Now, in order to tear down the things hiding in the darkness, we need strength. And how do we strengthen our bodies? With food and exercise. So, we are going to talk about those things now, spiritual food and exercise.

In Deuteronomy 8:3 we are told:

> 3 *He humbled you, causing you to hunger and then feeding you with manna, which neither you nor your ancestors had known, to teach you that man does not live on bread alone but on every word that comes from the mouth of the Lord.*

Man does not live by bread alone but by every word that comes from the mouth of God. There is our spiritual food... every word that comes from the mouth of God, better known as God's word or The Bible. We need to feed on God's word daily. As often as we sit to put food in our earthly bodies, we should also be feeding our spiritual bodies. We need to start our day with a little breakfast, a few verses to wake us up. A quick lunch later in the day, possibly a daily devotional to keep us focused. A big dinner, read a chapter or two or listen to a message from a favorite pastor to fill our bodies. A bedtime snack to put our mind at ease like a Psalm or Proverb.

Just like food is important to keep us strong, God's word is important to keep us strong as well. Jesus even says in John 6:35:

> ***35*** *Then Jesus declared, "I am the bread of life. Whoever comes to me will never go hungry, and whoever believes in me will never be thirsty.*

Jesus says that He is all the nourishment that we need. He is our food supply, and we shall never go hungry on His eternal supply.

Now, as towards exercising. We need to stay fit; we need to be in this for the long haul. I look at Hebrews 12:1-3 to start off:

> *Therefore, since we are surrounded by such a great cloud of witnesses, let us throw off*

> *everything that hinders and the sin that so easily entangles. And let us run with perseverance the race marked out for us,* **2** *fixing our eyes on Jesus, the pioneer and perfecter of faith. For the joy set before him he endured the cross, scorning its shame, and sat down at the right hand of the throne of God.* **3** *Consider him who endured such opposition from sinners, so that you will not grow weary and lose heart.*

We are running a race, the sin that we carry is a weight slowing us down, or a chain holding us back. We must rid ourselves of this so that we may be swift on our feet. And by keeping our focus on Jesus we can see that He has suffered more than we have, gone through more pain and suffering just so we can be with Him.

So, we need to prepare ourselves for this race, we need to work out and stay in shape. What better way to get in shape than joining a gym and getting a couple of workout buddies? What do I mean by this exactly? Join a church and surround yourselves with other believers. Proverbs 27:17 tells us the importance of workout buddies:

> **17** *As iron sharpens iron,*
> *so one person sharpens another.*

We need to be sharp, on our toes, and we can do it together. A friend will keep you accountable. They will push you beyond the limits you thought you had. They are there for you when you fall and can help you get back up and moving in the right direction. Friends are very important in your life. And the best place to find these friends is the church.

Jesus even tells us in Matthew 18:20:

> ***20*** *For where two or three gather in my name, there am I with them."*

So, when you are with a friend, or a bunch of them, Jesus is there with us. When we get together, for the purpose of worship and praise, Jesus is there with us. If we meet with some friends for coffee and Bible study, Jesus is there. If we go to a park and talk with a friend about what we have learned from the Bible, Jesus is there. If we meet with a preacher for one-on-one counseling, Jesus is there with us. And if there are more of us gathered, like say a church, Jesus is right there in our midst.

People have issues with the church, I mean it is filled with sinners after all. But we are all sinners in need of salvation. (Remember what Romans 3:23 said)

> ***23*** *for all have sinned and fall short of the glory of God,*

It does not have an exclusion for those in the church, ALL have sinned and fallen short. But the church is where we go to learn. The church is where we get stronger, exercising and building up our spiritual bodies. This is where we learn all about God's plan for us. (Books like this one are fine, but God already has an instruction manual for us, the Bible) The church is where we go to worship, praise, pray, mourn, lift up each other, learn, teach, preach, heal, get filled with God, and so much more. Church is where we go to learn how to change our sinful ways and how to become better children of God.

To show the importance of the church, let us look at Ephesians 5:23:

> **23** *For the husband is the head of the wife as Christ is the head of the church, his body, of which he is the Savior.*

The church, all of us sinners joined together, are the body of Jesus. He is the head, the brain, and we are the rest of the body. And without a head the body is dead, and without the body the head is powerless. We need to be whole, body and head.

Now, I do not want to point fingers, say one is better than others, or tell you where you must go. But there are some things you must check out for the churches you attend:

1. They MUST teach the Word of God. Not the Bible plus anything, only the Holy word of God.
2. They MUST teach that Jesus is the Son of God. Not that He was a great man, or a prophet. Not a teacher. Not anything other than God's Son.

3. They also MUST teach the resurrection. Jesus died and, if that were the end of it, we would not have salvation for our sins. Jesus lived, died, and was RAISED from the dead.
4. Jesus is the ONLY way to God. There is no Jesus and anything. Jesus is all you need.
5. Forgiveness is eternal. God does not break His promises. So, if He says that you have been forgiven, then you have been forgiven. You cannot lose the free gift God gave you.
6. As I have stated many times in this book, all have sinned, there are no righteous beings in this world. (As I always say, "There has only been one perfect person in this world, and we crucified Him.") so the church MUST accept ALL people no matter the sin, no matter the color, no matter what differences, they are loved by God and should be welcomed in the church.

The church is a gathering of believers (and nonbelievers looking for answers) gathered together to listen to God's teaching. It is a place where the Holy Spirit fills us and makes us stronger. It is our gym where we exercise and get stronger, but we get stronger together. (Do not forget to get a workout buddy)

Let Us Pray:

Lord God, I thank You for giving me strength, more strength than I ever thought was possible. You have made me strong by surrounding me with friends, family, brothers, and sisters that encourage me, strengthen me, lift me up, and sometimes help tear me down. You have filled my life with many workout buddies, and I praise You for them all. I also praise You for the nourishment that You have given me: the food that my spiritual body needs to survive, the nuggets of wisdom, the light snacks, the gourmet meals, and the all-I-can eat banquets that are found in Your Word. Help me Lord to digest what You feed me so that it will help me to grow and become stronger in You.

Gear Up

We are getting ready for our journey, so we must be properly attired for it. You do not go to an important interview in a jogging outfit, and you do not go on a mountain hike in a tuxedo, there are proper outfits for those occasions. And so, there is a proper outfit to be donned on this Journey. It is titled the "armor of God" and we MUST wear it on this journey. We are going to look at one passage for this section, Ephesians 6:10-18, I am going to put the whole passage here and then look at it piece by piece:

> ***10*** *Finally, be strong in the Lord and in his*
> *mighty power.* ***11*** *Put on the full armor of*
> *God, so that you can take your stand against*
> *the devil's schemes.* ***12*** *For our struggle is*
> *not against flesh and blood, but against the*

> *rulers, against the authorities, against the*
> *powers of this dark world and against the*
> *spiritual forces of evil in the heavenly realms.*
> **13** *Therefore put on the full armor of God, so*
> *that when the day of evil comes, you may be*
> *able to stand your ground, and after you have*
> *done everything, to stand.* **14** *Stand firm then,*
> *with the belt of truth buckled around your*
> *waist, with the breastplate of righteousness*
> *in place,* **15** *and with your feet fitted with the*
> *readiness that comes from the gospel of peace.*
> **16** *In addition to all this, take up the shield*
> *of faith, with which you can extinguish all*
> *the flaming arrows of the evil one.* **17** *Take*
> *the helmet of salvation and the sword of the*
> *Spirit, which is the word of God.*
>
> **18** *And pray in the Spirit on all occasions with*
> *all kinds of prayers and requests. With this in*
> *mind, be alert and always keep on praying for*
> *all the Lord's people.*

There is a lot mentioned here that we need to focus on, but for the purpose of this section we are just going to look at the armor itself (I will come back to this in a later chapter). This passage opens up by saying we are in a battle, and we need the proper outfit for that battle, our armor, so let us look at what it mentions.

Belt of truth

You will notice that each piece of our armor has a significant role in our armor. And we are going to start with the one thing that is going to hold it all together, the truth. Now in today's gear we are not wearing a toga or a flowing robe to be tied to us with a belt, but we are wearing pants that need to be held up with this belt. We cannot keep our gear in order if we keep trying to hold our pants up. So, we need a good belt, first and foremost. There is nothing better for keeping our pants on tight than the truth. If we stand firm in the truth, we cannot waiver, for the truth does not change and is firm. If we remain in the truth, wc can keep our head held high not trying to appease the left or the right because the truth is not going to side with just one, but all.

Breastplate of righteousness

Now, these are all terms for armor but for the purpose of this book I am going to try to make them into something needed for hiking/journeying, so I am going to TRY to redescribe these items. A breastplate protects the heart, so here we are going to consider it a jacket. We are protecting our heart, the lifeblood of our bodies, with the jacket, a heavy jacket to protect us from the elements we face on a daily basis. And that jacket is made of righteousness, our morals or what is right. We need to protect our hearts by doing what is right not only in the eyes of the world but what is right in the eyes of God. We know what He says is right and wrong, we need to focus on that to protect our hearts.

Shoes of the gospel of peace

Our shoes, which help us to keep our stability and traction on the path we are on. The verse mentions us having readiness with the gospel of peace. The peace we are talking about is the salvation we receive from Jesus the moment we ask for forgiveness of our sins. We have a firm foundation in our salvation, Psalm 40:1-2 says it like this:

> ***1*** *I waited patiently for the Lord;*
> *he turned to me and heard my cry.*
> ***2*** *He lifted me out of the slimy pit,*
> *out of the mud and mire;*
> *he set my feet on a rock*
> *and gave me a firm place to stand.*

He lifts us out of the slimy pit (our sin by way of His forgiveness) and places us on a rock, a solid place for our feet, a firm foundation that is our salvation in Him. Now, here we are discussing our footing, in a moment more on our salvation itself.

Shield of faith

A shield, our protection, for this outfit we are going to call it our backpack. This is where everything we need for the journey resides, our faith. Every time I discuss faith, I remember a witnessing study I did decades ago that taught me an acronym for faith:

F = Forgiveness of our sins
A = Available
I = Impossible
T = Turn (repent)
H = Heaven

So, putting it all together it becomes: Forgiveness is available, but it is impossible unless you turn towards heaven. This is the basis of our faith. That God loves us so much that He gave us His Son so that we can be made righteous. Without our faith in this, we are never going to be made holy in the sight of God. Without this assurance from our Father, we will NEVER make it to Him, for we are all sinners and unworthy. So, we carry all we need in our backpack of FAITH.

Helmet of salvation

Our heads need to be protected; without our heads our life is over. Not a helmet for us, but a hat to keep our heads protected. Salvation is defined as:

> "Preservation or deliverance from harm, ruin, or loss."

Our heads, our mindset, is that we are being delivered from sin/death. John 3:16-17 assures us of this:

> ***16*** *For God so loved the world that he gave his one and only Son, that whoever believes in him shall not perish but have eternal life.* ***17***
> *For God did not send his Son into the world to condemn the world, but to save the world through him.*

Above all that we are (as a hat is) is the fact that God loves us and wants us not to die as is the punishment of our sins, but instead wants us to be with Him so He gave us His Son. I always include verse 17 because it goes on to tell us Jesus did not come to condemn us (we were already condemned by the sin we have in our lives) but that we might be saved, rescued, delivered from the death we were in.

Sword of the spirit (the word of God)

The sword of the spirit, for our outfit, our walking stick. It will defeat all the predators we face. A walking stick can be swung like a bat at the enemies we face to ward them off. It also helps us stand when we are weary and tired. (Although a sword is not used in this fashion, it could be used to lean on). This walking stick is the Bible, it will, and already has, defeat all our enemies. It will give us peace, strength, rest, energy, and all the weaponry we need on this journey.

Prayer

Now why did I include this on the gear up section? Because this is also an important part of our gear. Prayer is our MAP, our GPS (Goal Positioning System, it is always directing us towards our goal- eternity with our Father), it is the communication we have with someone that not only has been on this path before (actually, He is right there with us), but it is also a roadmap to where we are going. We need to look at the map constantly to make certain we are not lost, we are not making a wrong turn somewhere, it is our guidance system for our journey.

Every day, multiple times a day, we need to look at the map. Every day, several times a day, we need to Talk to our Father who knows all the landmarks, twists, turns, hidden pathways, and dangers we will encounter on the way. Prayer is our important accessory, we need it when things are hard and we ask God to help get us through it, we need it when things look impossible and we need Him to help as only He can, we need it when things are good and we want to share what we see, we need it when things are amazing so we can tell Him how wonderful this journey really is. We need to:

1 Thessalonians 5:17-18
17 *pray continually,* ***18*** *give thanks in all circumstances; for this is God's will for you in Christ Jesus.*

Let Us Pray:

Lord, I praise You for giving us all that we need for this journey. The outfit You give us is all we need, the protection You provide is all we need, the Love You have for us is more than enough for all we are going through. I praise You, my God, for all that You have done for me, and I thank You for the forgiveness You have secured my life with.

Grow Up

Now, I do not mean to make this sound bad, but you do need to grow up. You cannot expect a "newborn" to immediately go out on a journey. You need to learn to walk, get better at it, and continue learning until you are good at it.

I have been writing a blog since late 2017 called: "Truth, Fully Spoken" on wordpress.com. One of the first posts I wrote (also one of the most popular ones) I entitled "Stages of a Christian's life", and it fits perfectly on this topic, so I am going to copy it here for you.

There are several stages of life: infancy, toddler, teenager, young adult, adult and senior. And there are just as many stages to Christian life, so I am going to attempt to explain them here using the verse John 3:16 (KJV):

> *16 For God so loved the world, that he gave his only begotten Son, that whosoever believeth on him should not perish, but have eternal life.*

So, let us take a look at Christianity here....

Christian Infancy

This is for new Christians, those that just gave their lives to Jesus and are beginning their walk with God. They may have HEARD of John 3:16, maybe they have seen the verse posted on a sign at a ballgame, it may even be the reason they repented and came to Christ. But their life has just begun, so they do not really know what the verse really says or means. They are newborns, so they must be fed the truth and cared for as they begin their new life.

Christian Toddler

As a toddler, we stumble, we crawl, we LEARN. It is at this stage in life that we learn the stories of the Bible, Noah, Abraham, Jesus (life, death, and resurrection), apostles etc... during this stage of our life we now have John 3:16 memorized and placed into our hearts. Sharing it everywhere we go. We are learning the basic truths of God's love for us, the truths we need to grow in God's love.

Christian Teenager

This is a tough time in our Christian life. This is where we usually rebel because we feel we know it all. This time in our lives has usually begun because of a turbulent time in our life, a time of sorrow, pain, loss of a loved one, something not going the way we expected, etc. So here we say, "if God loves the world, how could He allow this to happen?" This is a very trying time in our lives, but we can still mature and move forward. It is in this stage of life that we question our beliefs, we may even turn away from time to time, but God is still right there with us, God is still walking with us, God is still helping us mature.

Young Adult Christians

Now, we just came through a trying time in our life (the teenage stage), and realize God was there all the while. Standing beside us, guiding us, directing us, and PROTECTING us (mostly from ourselves) Here in our walk we learn new ways to communicate with those around us, so we learn new ways to say the same thing.

This is how I have been saying this verse, it is long but bear with me...

"For God so loved the world, wait a moment back in the 80s we had the song "we are the world" and I am part of we so that means... God so loved me, that He gave His only Son, wait again there... as Christians we believe in the trinity (Father, Son and Holy Ghost) and the three are one so that means that God so loved me that HE came so that whosoever (again that is me) believes in Him should not perish (that means die, and to die without God means to go to Hell) but have everlasting life (in Heaven with Him)".

So now let us relook at the whole verse my way... For God so loved me that He came here so that if I believe in Him, I will not die and go to hell but live life in heaven with Him for all eternity.

Adult Christians

Now we are maturing to a level of responsibility. We may have had roles in the church, but we were "going through the motions" doing them because we felt we had to. Now we are doing them because we are CALLED to. And in this stage of life, we start looking around the Bible to not just the one verse but others as well. I have always said John 3:17 (KJV) is more powerful than 16, (it is why they are both part of my email address):

> *17 For God sent not the Son into the world to judge the world; but that the world should be saved through him.*

See, this shows the REASON for vs 16... God did not come to condemn us but to SAVE us. and we need to know that more than anything. This is the verse that shows we are not worthy, but He saved us anyway.

Christian Seniors

These are the mentors of the Christian faith. These people look deeper into scripture noting the "how's", "why's", "where's", and "what for's" of verses. They can tell you who was being spoken to, what other verses pertain to this, how it pertains to you and me today. These are the ones that lead us and direct us properly.... Like Moses, Joseph, Job, Abraham, Ruth, etc.

What Stage Are You In? So here is a SIMPLE break down of Christian life, where do you fall in the spectrum? It is possible to be in several stages, a toddler acting like a teenager, or even a young adult acting like a toddler, but there is always one that is the "main" part of your Christian walk. I see myself more like a young adult, trying to mature to the next stage (I have a LOT of work to do personally before I would ever consider being that mature) But I want to point out a couple of quick notes here... every stage is important to the next. You must start as an infant, you must learn to walk, you WILL have a rebellious period, you WILL mature as you grow. just as it is important to be in each stage, it is important to help those below you. So teenagers can help toddlers (it is one of the ways teens become young adults, they realize their importance) Young adults can help teens and toddlers and usually the reason for so many infants in the family (no pun intended there) There are times when people feel comfortable in a stage, not wanting to mature in life (we see lots of Christians today in that "know-it-all" teen stage that will never grow up) as their mentors we need to help them grow AND love them enough to let them do it on their own. There is a reason for you to be where you are, you do not immediately go from an infant to an adult, (although many have tried to do just that.) MOST IMPORTANT FACT OF ALL THESE STAGES IS... you ARE a CHRISTIAN. Jesus has promised that once you accept Him, NOTHING or NOONE can take you away. So even as a rebellious teenager you are still a part (an IMPORTANT part) of the Christian Family! No matter which stage you are in, once you accept Jesus, you are part of God's family and that will never change.

Let Us Pray:

Lord, I praise You for accepting me into Your family. Lord, I thank You for the mentors You have placed in my life, and for helping me to mentor those younger Christians. I thank You for helping me grow, giving me the lessons in life that I need, the experience to help me learn, and the ability to mature in Your family. Lord, I ask that as I grow You direct me to younger, newer Christians that need my mentorship to help them grow in You.

Speak Up

Now, this section is not going to be what you think, it is not about vocalizing but showing your faith to the world. The way Christians do that is by baptism. There are differing opinions within the church dealing with baptism, and I am not going to argue the point today (or ever), but I am going to discuss what the Bible, God's word, says about it.

First, we have already said that all that is needed is faith, nothing else. Read Romans 10:9:

> **9** *If you declare with your mouth, "Jesus is Lord," and believe in your heart that God raised him from the dead, you will be saved.*

We are told right here that all we need to do is believe that Jesus is Lord God, and we are then saved. Baptism is not important to your salvation. And to prove this point we look to Jesus on the cross. We look to Luke 23:39-43:

> **39** *One of the criminals who hung their hurled insults at him: "Aren't you the Messiah? Save yourself and us!"*
>
> **40** *But the other criminal rebuked him. "Don't you fear God," he said, "since you are under the same sentence?* **41** *We are punished justly, for we are getting what our deeds deserve. But this man has done nothing wrong."*
>
> **42** *Then he said, "Jesus, remember me when you come into your kingdom."*
>
> **43** *Jesus answered him, "Truly I tell you, today you will be with me in paradise."*

There were two criminals that were crucified with Jesus both were guilty of their crimes and worthy of their punishment (I am not justifying the crucifixion as a punishment, but that was the punishment that was determined for them at that time). One was not sorry even to the moment of death, and the other defended Jesus, believed in Jesus, and asked for His forgiveness at the end. The point I always make here is that Jesus did not tell him to go and get baptized, He said "Today you will be with Me…" So, baptism is not important.

But we also need to look at the other aspect, the importance of baptism. For this we look at Jesus again. In Matthew 3:13-17, it says:

> **13** *Then Jesus came from Galilee to the Jordan to be baptized by John.* **14** *But John tried to deter him, saying, "I need to be baptized by you, and do you come to me?"*
>
> **15** *Jesus replied, "Let it be so now; it is proper for us to do this to fulfill all righteousness." Then John consented.*
>
> **16** *As soon as Jesus was baptized, he went up out of the water. At that moment heaven was opened, and he saw the Spirit of God descending like a dove and alighting on him.*
> **17** *And a voice from heaven said, "This is my Son, whom I love; with him I am well pleased."*

Jesus, at the beginning of His ministry, came to John to be baptized. But John already knew who Jesus was and said that Jesus should baptize John instead. Jesus said that He needed to be baptized to fulfill all righteousness. Baptism is a washing away, a cleansing, a rebirth from our old self and into a new holy life with God. Jesus did not need to be cleansed of His sin, (He was sinless, perfect, without blemish because He was God's Son), but He needed to be baptized so that He fulfilled all the "requirements" of the LAW (at this time, He had not died so His sacrifice had not brought the new covenant into existence yet), and because He was starting His missionary work.

So, baptism is not an important part of your salvation, BUT it is an important part of your walk because it shows the world that you have been reborn, you have been cleansed, your sins have been washed away and you have been made righteous. Baptism is a public profession of your faith in Jesus, the start of your journey with God in the right direction.

Let Us Pray:

My God, I know that You have forgiven my sins, and I know that is all that is "required" but I want the world to know the changes that You have made in my life. Let Your light shine through me so that the entire world may see You in me. Lord, I thank You for the example You have provided me through the life and ministry of Jesus here on Earth, and I ask that You help me to be like Christ in my walk. Lord, help me to show the world that You are indeed in me, with me, and working through me each and every day.

Step Up

Ok, we have our outfits on, we have grown to a mature age, gotten stronger, and even have a few workout buddies to help us along the way. It is now time to go. We are even told to do so in Matthew 28:18-20:

> ***18*** *Then Jesus came to them and said, "All*
> *authority in heaven and on earth has been*
> *given to me.* ***19*** *Therefore go and make*
> *disciples of all nations, baptizing them in*
> *the name of the Father and of the Son and*
> *of the Holy Spirit,* ***20*** *and teaching them to*
> *obey everything I have commanded you. And*
> *surely I am with you always, to the very end*
> *of the age."*

We are ready to go and teach, go and obey, go and do as we have been commanded by God, go with God by our side.

Please do not be afraid, look at Hebrews 13:5-8:

> **5** *Keep your lives free from the love of money and be content with what you have, because God has said,*
> *"Never will I leave you;*
> *never will I forsake you."*
>
> **6** *So we say with confidence,*
> *"The Lord is my helper; I will not be afraid.*
> *What can mere mortals do to me?"*
>
> **7** *Remember your leaders, who spoke the*
> *word of God to you. Consider the outcome*
> *of their way of life and imitate their faith.* **8**
> *Jesus Christ is the same yesterday and today*
> *and forever.*

God has made us several promises here and we need to place these promises close to our hearts, and subject them to our memories.

First of all, He will never leave us. No matter where we go, God is right there with us. This is an extremely important thing to remember as we go along the way (the next chapter) We are never alone, we are never left to our own devices, we will always have God by our side.

God promises to never forsake us. Look at the definition of the word forsake from dictionary.com:

> "to quit or leave entirely; abandon; desert."

These are what God promises us He will never do. He will never quit on us; we are His always no matter what. He will never leave us, even when we try to hide from Him (which we can never do FYI) He will NEVER abandon us, even when we are at our lowest God is there with us. And how do we know this? Because He promises us that.

Another promise here is that He is our helper. When we are in distress, He is there (right there with us) to help us out. When we are in need, He is there to help provide what is needed. When we are confused or in need of wisdom, He is there with the answers we need to help us figure out the questions we have.

If God is right there with us, if God will not desert us, if God has promised to help us then what can any human being ever do to harm us. This is stated another way in Romans 8:31-32:

> ***31*** *What, then, shall we say in response to these things? If God is for us, who can be against us?* ***32*** *He who did not spare his own Son, but gave him up for us all—how will he not also, along with him, graciously give us all things?*

And then we are also told in Romans 8:38-39:

> **38** *For I am convinced that neither death nor life, neither angels nor demons, neither the present nor the future, nor any powers,* **39**
> *neither height nor depth, nor anything else in all creation, will be able to separate us from the love of God that is in Christ Jesus our Lord.*

There is nothing in or around this world that can separate us from God, NOTHING. God will never leave us, and if He is with us then nothing can take us away from Him. This is His promise to us, His children, and God ALWAYS keeps His promises.

Let Us Pray:

Thank You God for not abandoning me, thank You for never quitting on me, thank You for being with me even at my lowest. God, I praise You for standing by me even though I do not deserve it, for holding onto me tight and not letting go. I praise You, Jesus, for making me part of Your family and preparing me for the journey that is ahead of me.

Listen Up

I already mentioned the map we are using to guide us along the way, we could consider it a GPS. A guidance system to help us along our way. The thing with a GPS though is we need to listen to it. It tells us where to go, how to get there, the easiest way to get to our destination, and sometimes it even tells us about hazards on the way. The map I said was prayer, and prayer is talking to our Father, who happens to be the one that made the path we are on, perfected the map, even created the GPS (and all of our other gear) that we are using. So, when He speaks to us, we need to listen.

For this section, let us look at someone God spoke to that did NOT listen at first (and a few other times): Jonah. God told Jonah to go to Nineveh and tell them that their sinful ways were going to destroy them, soon, but Jonah did not want to go. Jonah 1:1-2 begins with:

> *The word of the LORD came to Jonah son of Amittai:* **2** *"Go to the great city of Nineveh and preach against it, because its wickedness has come up before me."*

Instead, Jonah decided to go in the opposite direction by way of boat. Jonah 1:3 continues:

> **3** *But Jonah ran away from the LORD and headed for Tarshish. He went down to Joppa, where he found a ship bound for that port. After paying the fare, he went aboard and sailed for Tarshish to flee from the LORD.*

Trying to hide from God, Jonah stayed below on the boat, but you cannot hide from God. And God rocked the boat until it almost fell apart. Jonah 1:4:

> **4** *Then the LORD sent a great wind on the sea, and such a violent storm arose that the ship threatened to break up.*

The crew on the boat got scared and sacrificed all they could to their gods to no avail. Then they turned to Jonah, and he told them he was running from what the One true God wanted him to do. They pleaded with him to appease his God so that they might live. Jonah had them throw him overboard and immediately God calmed the waters, sent a gigantic fish to swallow Jonah for three days, and deliver him to Nineveh (This is the rest of Jonah chapter 1).

Once in Nineveh, Jonah preached in their streets that God was going to destroy them in 40 days. The entire town repented, and God forgave them (Jonah chapter 3).

Now, if Jonah had just listened to God in the first place, none of the hardship would have happened, and he would have accomplished what God wanted him to do.

On the other hand, we have Moses, who when God spoke to him did what was told of him. There are many examples to use for this, but I am going to use the example of the Red Sea.

Moses was leading the Hebrews out of Egypt (as God had instructed him) when they arrived at the Red Sea. The Egyptians were closing in, and the sea was before them. God told Moses to hold up his staff and the waters would part so that they would cross on dry land. Moses listened to God, the sea parted, and they crossed the Red Sea on dry land. This is from Exodus 14:15-16:

> ***15*** *Then the LORD said to Moses, "Why are you crying out to me? Tell the Israelites to move on.* ***16*** *Raise your staff and stretch out your hand over the sea to divide the water so that the Israelites can go through the sea on dry ground.*

See, God will direct us to where we need to go, as long as we listen to Him and follow His instructions. This is not always easy because, like Jonah, we may not want to do what He tells us to, or we think we know better, or a better way to do it. Sometimes we need to listen closely because God is speaking to us in a whisper. 1 Kings 19:11-13 reminds us:

> **11** *The Lord said, "Go out and stand on the mountain in the presence of the Lord, for the Lord is about to pass by."*
>
> *Then a great and powerful wind tore the mountains apart and shattered the rocks before the Lord, but the Lord was not in the wind. After the wind there was an earthquake, but the Lord was not in the earthquake.* **12**
> *After the earthquake came a fire, but the Lord was not in the fire. And after the fire came a gentle whisper.* **13** *When Elijah heard it, he pulled his cloak over his face and went out and stood at the mouth of the cave.*
>
> *Then a voice said to him, "What are you doing here, Elijah?"*

Sometimes with a loud voice like in Matthew 3:16-17:

> **16** *As soon as Jesus was baptized, he went up out of the water. At that moment heaven*

> *was opened, and he saw the Spirit of God descending like a dove and alighting on him.*
> **17** *And a voice from heaven said, "This is my Son, whom I love; with him I am well pleased."*

Sometimes with no spoken word at all as in Daniel 5:5-6:

> **5** *Suddenly the fingers of a human hand appeared and wrote on the plaster of the wall, near the lampstand in the royal palace. The king watched the hand as it wrote.* **6** *His face turned pale and he was so frightened that his legs became weak and his knees were knocking.*

But He is speaking to us letting us know where we need to be going on our journey.

Let Us Pray:

Lord, God, help me to hear Your voice. Help me to discern what You are telling me and help me to follow Your instructions. Let me know when I have made a wrong turn and help me to get back on the right path. Lord, Your word promises me that You have plans for me of good, help me to see Your plans, and follow Your words so that I continue to go in the direction You have for me.

The Hike

So, now that we are prepared for the hike, let us take a look at the path we are going to be on. The pathway is not paved, it is not going to be smooth and even, it is not even going to be straight, there will be twists, turns, and even a wrong turn or two along the way, but the path leads us towards our final goal- the throne room of our Father. There are hills to climb, valleys to cross, dark corners, and peaceful meadows all along the way, and the entire time God is right with us step by step.

So, we need to look at where we are going. Look at what God has promised for us in Deuteronomy 8:1-5:

> *Be careful to follow every command I am giving you today, so that you may live and increase and may enter and possess the land*

the Lord promised on oath to your ancestors.
2 *Remember how the Lord your God led*
you all the way in the wilderness these forty
years, to humble and test you in order to
know what was in your heart, whether or
not you would keep his commands. **3** *He*
humbled you, causing you to hunger and
then feeding you with manna, which neither
you nor your ancestors had known, to teach
you that man does not live on bread alone
but on every word that comes from the
mouth of the Lord. **4** *Your clothes did not*
wear out and your feet did not swell during
these forty years. **5** *Know then in your heart*
that as a man disciplines his son, so the Lord
your God disciplines you.

First thing to note is God has led you this far, He has brought you through the wilderness to this point. You have been fed, clothed, and cared for even before you accepted Him and became His child. He has tested your heart to make certain where your true faith lies. And He is bringing you into the land He has promised you.

Deuteronomy 8:6-9 describes the land we are promised:

6 *Observe the commands of the Lord your*
God, walking in obedience to him and
revering him. **7** *For the Lord your God is*

> *bringing you into a good land—a land with brooks, streams, and deep springs gushing out into the valleys and hills;* **8** *a land with wheat and barley, vines and fig trees, pomegranates, olive oil and honey;* **9** *a land where bread will not be scarce and you will lack nothing; a land where the rocks are iron and you can dig copper out of the hills.*

The land, reserved for those that obey His commands, is described here as a good land with refreshing water, delicious food (and plenty of it) and full of all we will ever need.

Deuteronomy 8:10 reminds us:

> **10** *When you have eaten and are satisfied, praise the Lord your God for the good land he has given you.*

to praise Him for this land he has given us.

In Psalm 23 we are also told about the path we are on:

> **1** *The Lord is my shepherd, I lack nothing.*
> **2** *He makes me lie down in green pastures,*
> *he leads me beside quiet waters,*
> **3** *he refreshes my soul.*
> *He guides me along the right paths*

for his name's sake.
4 *Even though I walk*
through the darkest valley,
I will fear no evil,
for you are with me;
your rod and your staff,
they comfort me.
5 *You prepare a table before me*
in the presence of my enemies.
You anoint my head with oil;
my cup overflows.
6 *Surely your goodness and love will follow me*
all the days of my life,
and I will dwell in the house of the LORD
forever.

There are green pastures, quiet waters, and even dark valleys. He guides us on the right paths (but sometimes we go the wrong way)

Another thing I want to point out here is that He has to make us rest, He must tell us to relax along the way. We are going along the path with meadows, brooks, rivers, trees, flowers and scenery, and God has to tell us to stop and smell the roses.

Let Us Pray:

God, I thank You for guiding me along the pathway of my life. I thank You for the meadows, the brooks, the flowers, and the other scenes that You have provided for me. Help me to stop and rest along the way, to enjoy what You have provided for me.

Hills

Now we are going to look at some of the things we are going to experience on our journey. Starting with the hills (and sometimes mountains) we will face.

Life sometimes is an uphill battle. There are struggles that we will have and every step we take is treacherous. The first three verses of Psalm 73 say this:

> ***1*** *Surely God is good to Israel,*
> *to those who are pure in heart.*
> ***2*** *But as for me, my feet had almost slipped;*
> *I had nearly lost my foothold.*
> ***3*** *For I envied the arrogant*
> *when I saw the prosperity of the wicked.*

See, we all slip and stumble, lose our footing along the way. Here the psalmist even says why he nearly lost his footing, because he looked at the prosperity of the sinners. He took his eyes off God, and God's direction, and did not pay attention to where he was going. This is a problem we all have; we climb the hills in front of us and then take our eyes off our path and almost lose our footing (more on this to come).

But once we get to the top, we are on cloud nine. The view is amazing. When we focus on God, we can make it to the top.

Look at Psalm 18:30-32:

> **30** *As for God, his way is perfect:*
> *The Lord's word is flawless;*
> *he shields all who take refuge in him.*
> **31** *For who is God besides the Lord?*
> *And who is the Rock except our God?*
> **32** *It is God who arms me with strength*
> *and keeps my way secure.*

And continued in verse 36:

> **36** *You provide a broad path for my feet,*
> *so that my ankles do not give way.*

God's way is perfect, secure, flawless, and broad. His way helps us to get to the top of the hill (or mountain) where the view is awesome, just like the God we worship that helped us get there.

Let Us Pray:

God, sometimes the road is steep and hard, but You are there to help me make it to the top. When I keep my eyes focused on You the path is broad and safe, when I take my eyes off of You though, I slip, stumble, and sometimes fall. Help Me, Lord, to keep my eyes focused on You and Your ways.

Valleys

Once we leave the mountaintop it is all downhill from there. We end up heading towards the valleys. Remember how Psalm 23 described it in verse 4?

> 4 *Even though I walk*
> *through the darkest valley,*
> *I will fear no evil,*
> *for you are with me;*
> *your rod and your staff,*
> *they comfort me.*

Now, look how the NKJV (New King James Version) states it:

> 4 *Yea, though I walk through the valley of the*
> *shadow of death,*

I will fear no evil;
For You are with me;
Your rod and Your staff, they comfort me

The valley of the shadow of death. The valleys are low points, the lowest points on our journey. Psalm 71:19-20 lets us know:

19 *Your righteousness, God, reaches to the heavens,*
you who have done great things.
Who is like you, God?
20 *Though you have made me see troubles, many and bitter,*
you will restore my life again;
from the depths of the earth
you will again bring me up.

We always think of God in the heavens, but He is there with us in the depths, in the valleys of our lives where we feel like death has surrounded us, and there He can still lift us up and restore us. He can still lead us out of this dark valley, this pit of despair and sadness, and back to the joy and peace He has waiting for us.

It is hard to focus in the valleys when we are surrounded by the shadows. It is hard to remember that God is by our side when we are in the depression of our journey. But God is there waiting for us to remember, protecting us from the death that surrounds us in the valley. And He will restore us and aid us back up the hill towards the next mountaintop.

Let Us Pray:

God, when I am in the valleys of my life comfort me. When I am in the depression that encompasses me in those valleys, I ask that You surround me and protect me from the shadows. I Praise You, Father, for standing by my side even within the valleys of my life.

Meadows

Remember the meadows and brooks mentioned in Psalm 23? They are our rest stops. God makes us stop and relax, God knows we are rushing and always in a hurry. So, we can get tired, feel run down, overburdened, or stressed and the best cure for that is resting. Jesus tells us in Matthew 11:28-29:

> ***28*** *"Come to me, all you who are weary and burdened, and I will give you rest.* ***29*** *Take my yoke upon you and learn from me, for I am gentle and humble in heart, and you will find rest for your souls.*

If we are tired, burdened by the weight we carry, stressed, anxious, depressed, or just out of energy all we need to do is go to Him and He will give us the rest we need. He will reenergize us; He will help us relax, He will make us lie down in green pastures and relax by the calming brook. For as long as we need to be there. God does not want us stressed out, because we are no good in that condition, we need our energy so that we can make it all the way on our journey.

The road is long, but God gives us these rest stops along the way filled with beauty and peace to calm our spirit, ease our minds, and relax our souls. There is plenty of food and water in these stops to help us refresh our spirits, strengthen our minds, and renew our bodies for the road ahead. So, enjoy the meadows when they come along because they are there for your enjoyment and benefit.

Let Us Pray:

Thank You, Jesus, for giving me the rest that I need, the break that I deserve, and the peace of mind that is provided within the meadows. Lord, help me to relax and enjoy these areas that You have provided for me. Yes, the road is long, but these rest areas are provided for me by You so that I may finish the course set before me.

Wrong Turns

Now it is time to talk about the path we are on, and some of the obstacles along the way. The first one to discuss are the wrong turns we make along the way. I want to say thanks to our GPS that this never happens, but we do not listen to the GPS all the time because we think we know best (even though our guide has been down this path we still believe we know better.) So, sometimes we make a wrong turn and head in the wrong direction.

James 4:1-3 says:

> *What causes fights and quarrels among you? Don't they come from your desires that battle within you?* **2** *You desire but do not have, so you kill. You covet but you cannot get what you want, so you quarrel and fight. You do*

> *not have because you do not ask God.* **3** *When you ask, you do not receive, because you ask with wrong motives, that you may spend what you get on your pleasures.*

What causes the strife between us? Wrong motives, wrong desires, wrong decisions, even wrong ideas, these are all ways of saying a wrong turn. Look at what James is saying, these things, these wrong turns we take, are because we turn from what God provided for us and want more selfish things for our lives. We desire what we do not have (envy), we covet what we do not get (lust), we do not ask God for the things He has for us instead we take what we believe we should have (stealing), and we do all of this because we have the wrong motives. The motive we have is "self" our pleasure, our desires, our benefit even though God provides all we will ever need to survive on our journey.

When we focus on ourselves, we take our eyes off of God and look at ourselves, we plug our ears and do not listen to our GPS and so we make a wrong turn. But the promise that we have is that even when we go the wrong way God is still there ready to direct us back to the right direction. We know this because as we have already discussed, God will never leave us nor forsake us because we are His children. Deuteronomy 31:6 tells us:

> **6** *Be strong and courageous. Do not be afraid or terrified because of them, for the Lord your*

God goes with you; he will never leave you nor forsake you."

No matter what, even when we take a wrong turn, God will be there with us and will never quit on us, leave us nor abandon us.

Let Us Pray:

Lord, I often take my eyes off of You and make a wrong turn (or two, or three hundred). I know that even when I do go the wrong way that You are with me still protecting me and ready to guide me back to the path I was to be on. You stand by me ready to take me back to the right direction each and every time I turn the wrong way. Lord, remind me when I do make a wrong turn that You are near ready, willing, and able to lead me back onto the right path.

Trips

There are times when we trip over our own two feet. We are walking along and are not paying attention to the path we are on. And suddenly we trip, it is nothing serious, just a little trip, we might skin our knee or get a small bruise, but it is nothing to worry about. Matthew 26:41 warns us:

> ***41*** *"Watch and pray so that you will not fall into temptation. The spirit is willing, but the flesh is weak."*

We must continually watch out and pray that we do not fall (trip for my scenario) into temptation. Temptation is all around us, distracting us and making us fall. We are constantly wanting to follow God, but our flesh has its own plans. That is where we get into trouble here, our flesh wants pleasure right now and takes our eyes off the things we are supposed to be focused on- the pathway to God in heaven.

So, we slip and fall, but we get back up and keep going, after all this is just a little trip, not like we stumbled and hurt anything (next chapter). And with the help of our workout buddies, we can just dust ourselves off and continue on our way.

Let Us Pray:

God, I know that I am going to trip up and fall, but You are right there to catch me and place me back on track, thank You. Lord I ask now that You help me to keep my eyes focused on You and help me to avoid the temptations out there. I praise You, Father, for giving me friends to help me when I fall, for with their help I am able to stand back up and continue walking on my life's path.

Stumbles

Sometimes we do a little more than trip, sometimes we actually stumble and fall (flat on my face if it were me) And here we actually may need some help getting back up. Without someone to help us we are like the people described in Psalm 107:10-13:

> **10** *Some sat in darkness, in utter darkness,*
> *prisoners suffering in iron chains,*
> **11** *because they rebelled against God's commands*
> *and despised the plans of the Most High.*
> **12** *So he subjected them to bitter labor;*
> *they stumbled, and there was no one to help.*
> **13** *Then they cried to the* LORD *in their trouble,*
> *and he saved them from their distress.*

They were in darkness (sin) because the rebelled against God. So, they stumbled and fell in the darkness. That makes it even worse, they were in darkness and could not get back up, and they had no one to help them. Now, they cried out to God, and He did help them, but let us look at the other aspect… someone to help.

I mentioned earlier going to the gym (church) and having some workout buddies (friends to help you get stronger) this is where they come in handy. WHEN you stumble in the darkness, if you have some workout buddies, they can help lift you up and get back on your feet, it is called encouragement. 1 Thessalonians 5:11 tells us:

> **11** *Therefore encourage one another and build each other up, just as in fact you are doing.*

We need to encourage one another. We need to be there for our friends when they fall, and they should be there to help us when we fall. And 2 Corinthians 13:11 reminds us:

> **11** *Finally, brothers and sisters, rejoice! Strive for full restoration, encourage one another, be of one mind, live in peace. And the God of love and peace will be with you.*

Strive for full restoration (healing) encourage one another and be of one mind. And one other way to state it is Proverbs 27:17:

17 As iron sharpens iron,
so one person sharpens another.

We need friends around us to keep us sharp (focused on God).

Let Us Pray:

God, I know that I will stumble and fall, help me to surround myself with brothers and sisters that will encourage me, pick me up, and keep me sharp and focused on what is important in my life, You.

Potholes

Sometimes we do not see the sin we are in; these are the potholes in our pathway. They are big, deep holes in the road that sneak up on us and they can hurt us when we hit them. We need to avoid these potholes whenever possible, but we are blinded by our own sin. Our brothers and sisters see them in us, and they can point out the potholes to us.

Matthew 18:15-17 tells us what to do when we see sin in others:

> ***15*** *"If your brother or sister sins, go and point*
> *out their fault, just between the two of you. If*
> *they listen to you, you have won them over.*
> ***16*** *But if they will not listen, take one or two*
> *others along, so that 'every matter may be*
> *established by the testimony of two or three*

> *witnesses.'* **17** *If they still refuse to listen, tell it to the church; and if they refuse to listen even to the church, treat them as you would a pagan or a tax collector.*

This is how potholes get spotted, and eventually fixed. When you see sin in someone, go to them in private and point it out. So, if someone comes to you and points out an issue you need to pay attention because they are trying to help you out. When potholes are spotted, they can be filled in and smoothed out.

Paul, one of the main writers in the New Testament, wrote in 1 Timothy 1:12-16:

> **12** *I thank Christ Jesus our Lord, who has given me strength, that he considered me trustworthy, appointing me to his service.*
> **13** *Even though I was once a blasphemer and a persecutor and a violent man, I was shown mercy because I acted in ignorance and unbelief.* **14** *The grace of our Lord was poured out on me abundantly, along with the faith and love that are in Christ Jesus.*

> **15** *Here is a trustworthy saying that deserves full acceptance: Christ Jesus came into the world to save sinners—of whom I am the worst.* **16** *But for that very reason I was shown*

> *mercy so that in me, the worst of sinners, Christ Jesus might display his immense patience as an example for those who would believe in him and receive eternal life.*

He was a sinner, according to him the worst sinner in the world. But the sins were pointed out to him so that he could change those behaviors (I will point out that the one who pointed his sins out to him was Jesus, but he was shown those sins none the less). Because he changed his behavior, he became a great man of God and a missionary to the Gentiles.

But there are times when we do not pay attention to the advice of our friends, and the scripture tells us what to do. We read it just a moment ago, Matthew 18:16-17:

> **16** *But if they will not listen, take one or two*
> *others along, so that 'every matter may be*
> *established by the testimony of two or three*
> *witnesses.'* **17** *If they still refuse to listen, tell*
> *it to the church; and if they refuse to listen*
> *even to the church, treat them as you would*
> *a pagan or a tax collector.*

Next, we bring one or two others with us to address the sin, and if they still do not listen take it before the church. See, if we are unwilling to change harmful behavior, then our heart has not changed. God loves you and will always forgive you, but you must be willing to give up your sinful ways. If you do not give them up, then you are unwilling to truly follow God and His ways (your desires and sins are more important). Jesus tells us in Matthew 6:24:

> **24** *"No one can serve two masters. Either you will hate the one and love the other, or you will be devoted to the one and despise the other. You cannot serve both God and money.*

We cannot follow God and sin at the same time. If we try to follow God and continue to sin, we will fall into the potholes. If we take care of the sin, we have then filled in the pothole and can continue to go on our path.

Let Us Pray:

God, there are many potholes on the road, there are millions of stumbling blocks in my path, help me to see them, avoid them and fix them so that I might continue following You closely. Thank You God, for forgiving me the worst of sinners. For without Your forgiveness, I could not have even begun this journey, let alone make it as far as I have.

Traps And Snares

I have mentioned our blunders, the trips and stumbling and even the potholes, but there are other problems to watch out for. The enemy has gone before us and set out traps and snares for us to fall into. These are called temptations, things our egos desire that we would turn our heads (and hearts).

To show us these traps, Jesus was tempted by Satan in the wilderness, beginning in Matthew 4:1:

> *Then Jesus was led by the Spirit into the wilderness to be tempted by the devil.*

The chapter tells us all the things Satan used to tempt Jesus the first was food in Matthew 4:2-3 (NIV):

> *2 After fasting forty days and forty nights, he was hungry. 3 The tempter came to him and said, "If you are the Son of God, tell these stones to become bread."*

Jesus was hungry, He had a desire to care for His body, and Satan tempted Him with food. The best answer to any temptation is scripture as in Matthew 4:4:

> *4 Jesus answered, "It is written: 'Man shall not live on bread alone, but on every word that comes from the mouth of God.'"*

The next temptation Satan used has to deal with protection (Matthew 4:5-7):

> *5 Then the devil took him to the holy city and had him stand on the highest point of the temple. 6 "If you are the Son of God," he said, "throw yourself down. For it is written:*
> *"'He will command his angels concerning you,*
> *and they will lift you up in their hands,*
> *so that you will not strike your foot against a stone.'"*
> *7 Jesus answered him, "It is also written: 'Do not put the Lord your God to the test.'"*

And the final part (Matthew 4:8-10) deals with our desires:

> *8 Again, the devil took him to a very high*
> *mountain and showed him all the kingdoms*
> *of the world and their splendor. 9 "All this I*
> *will give you," he said, "if you will bow down*
> *and worship me."*
>
> *10 Jesus said to him, "Away from me, Satan!*
> *For it is written: 'Worship the Lord your God*
> *and serve him only.'"*

Satan tempts us with things such as these, things to "care" for our lives, things to "protect" our lives even things to make us "powerful" or "worshipped". There is a problem here though, these things are not his to give. Anything he offers is fleeting and useless, only God can give us what we need, and He gives it to us freely.

Satan has placed many traps and snares in our path. And the best way to avoid them is with scripture in our heart. And this is a passage to memorize, James 4:7-8:

> *7 Submit yourselves, then, to God. Resist the*
> *devil, and he will flee from you. 8 Come near*
> *to God and he will come near to you. Wash*
> *your hands, you sinners, and purify your*
> *hearts, you double-minded.*

Resist the devil and he MUST flee. You are a child of God, he hates that, you are protected by God, he wants you to forget that. God loves you and is with you, and Satan wants you to ignore that. But nothing he can do will take you away from God, and that has been promised to you in Romans 8:38-39:

> **38** *For I am convinced that neither death nor life, neither angels nor demons, neither the present nor the future, nor any powers,* **39** *neither height nor depth, nor anything else in all creation, will be able to separate us from the love of God that is in Christ Jesus our Lord.*

Let Us Pray:

Lord protect me from the traps and snares placed before me by the enemy. Help me to avoid those traps and snares. Help me, God, to remember Your word and promises, help me to remember Your love for me, and help me to remember that there is nothing that can separate me from You.

Enjoy Your Time

Let me start this chapter with a verse Psalm 13:5-6:

> **5** *But I trust in your unfailing love;*
> *my heart rejoices in your salvation.*
> **6** *I will sing the* L*ORD's praise,*
> *for he has been good to me.*

This should be done daily, rejoice, sing, and praise towards God. God has done remarkable things for us, and we should praise Him for that. These two verses speak volumes on that, look at what God has done in these two verses, He loves us, He saves us, and He is good to us. What more do we need? All we need is freely given to us, rejoice in how much God loves us.

We just read Matthew 4:10 where Jesus told Satan:

> *10 Jesus said to him, "Away from me, Satan! For it is written: 'Worship the Lord your God and serve him only.'"*

We are to worship God only (trust me there is no one else worthy of our worship or praise) Psalm 146:1-3 tells us:

> *1 Praise the LORD.*
> *Praise the LORD, my soul.*
> *2 I will praise the LORD all my life;*
> *I will sing praise to my God as long as I live.*
> *3 Do not put your trust in princes,*
> *in human beings, who cannot save.*

Praise the Lord oh my soul all the days of my life. There are no kings, presidents, princes, parliaments, government or any other being that can save our souls.

Philippians 4:4-8 states this:

> *4 Rejoice in the Lord always. I will say it again:*
> *Rejoice! 5 Let your gentleness be evident to*
> *all. The Lord is near. 6 Do not be anxious*
> *about anything, but in every situation,*
> *by prayer and petition, with thanksgiving,*
> *present your requests to God. 7 And the peace*
> *of God, which transcends all understanding,*
> *will guard your hearts and your minds in*
> *Christ Jesus.*

> *8 Finally, brothers and sisters, whatever is true, whatever is noble, whatever is right, whatever is pure, whatever is lovely, whatever is admirable—if anything is excellent or praiseworthy—think about such things.*

Rejoice in God always, so much so we should say it again, **REJOICE!** In every situation (even in the valleys and potholes) we should give thanks. The good things we see, praise God for He is good. The bad we experience, praise God for He will protect us through it. The health we enjoy, thank God for our good days. The sickness we go through, praise God for His healing hands for He can provide the medical treatments and doctors to care for us. The temptations we go through, praise God for with Him the devil cannot touch us and must flee from us.

God has good plans for us, God is with us always, and God loves us even though we are sinners and unworthy. So, I say praise Him, and rejoice, again I say **REJOICE!**

Let Us Pray:

Lord, God, my Father I praise You for all that You have done. I worship You, and You alone, for You are the only one who can provide salvation. I rejoice in the knowledge that even in my troubled times, even when I do not deserve it, You love me and forgive me. Lord I rejoice now and always, my heart leaps with joy at the miracles You have performed in my life.

The Journey Continues

Let us look over what we have discussed in this book, the many nuggets we have discussed. Yes, I am going to use this chapter to summarize what we have learned.

We are on a journey and have made certain that we are going in the right direction. After we took the first step, that step of asking God to forgive our sins and accept us as we are, we have learned the next steps that we need to take.

We need to allow God's light to shine in us so that we can see what is hiding in the shadows of our lives. We need to get stronger by joining a gym (church) and getting some workout buddies (friends to keep us accountable). We need to make sure we have all the right gear on, and we have our

GPS with us. We need to mature and make certain we are prepared for the journey ahead of us. We need to speak up and publicly proclaim our love for God through baptism. And we need to learn to listen to God's voice (our GPS) in the many ways He speaks to us.

We are going on a journey. A path that will go up hills, where we might struggle but we will get to the top. The valleys below can be deadly with the shadows that they have, but God is there with us even at our lowest points. There are rest areas on the way, places where God gives us moments to rest, relax and reenergize our lives so that we have the strength to carry on.

There are many hazards on our way. Wrong turns that we may take, but our GPS will get us back on track when we use it. We will trip when we take our eyes off God and His plans for us. We will stumble and fall but with the encouragement and the help of our friends we can get back up, dust ourselves off and continue moving towards our final goal. But there are the potholes along the way too, those spots that we need to fix to smooth the pathway, but sometimes we do not see them and need the help of our friends to see them and fix them. Do not forget about the traps and snares the enemy has placed on the pathway either, they are dangerous and harmful, but because God is with us the enemy's schemes will not work and he must leave from us.

And, finally, we need to be happy, rejoice, sing songs of praise, and worship the only One worthy of our praise and worship, our Father. God has done great things for us, He has loved us, forgiven us, cared for us, and shown us grace and mercy. So, in good times and bad times we must rejoice.

Let Us Pray:

Lord, I praise You for this journey. You have been with me the entire way, and You will be with me the entire time I am on this journey. Thank You for Your love, Your forgiveness, Your grace, and mercy, for without those I would be lost and alone on the journey of my life. Thank You Father, for with Your help I am on this journey, with Your children's help I will be picked up when I fall. And with the GPS I may feel lost and confused, but You will always lead me back to the pathway I am going on.

The Last Step

There is one last step, the final step we take on our journey. Jesus tells us in John 14:1-4:

> *"Do not let your hearts be troubled. You believe in God; believe also in me.* **2** *My Father's house has many rooms; if that were not so, would I have told you that I am going there to prepare a place for you?* **3** *And if I go and prepare a place for you, I will come back and take you to be with me that you also may be where I am.* **4** *You know the way to the place where I am going."*

Jesus has gone before us to make ready the place we are going so that where He is we may be able to go as well.

Jesus died so that we could begin this journey, He rose from the dead so that our sins could be forgiven, and He has prepared our final destination so that it will be ready for when we finally make it to where He is: Heaven.

Hebrews 12:1-3 best sums up this whole book:

> *Therefore, since we are surrounded by such*
> *a great cloud of witnesses, let us throw off*
> *everything that hinders and the sin that*
> *so easily entangles. And let us run with*
> *perseverance the race marked out for us,*
> **2** *fixing our eyes on Jesus, the pioneer and*
> *perfecter of faith. For the joy set before him he*
> *endured the cross, scorning its shame, and sat*
> *down at the right hand of the throne of God.*
> **3** *Consider him who endured such opposition*
> *from sinners, so that you will not grow weary*
> *and lose heart.*

We are running a race per this passage, but it is more like a journey of time. The path has been laid out for us and we need to throw away all that may hinder, entangle, or ensnare us (sin and temptation). We need to keep our eyes on Jesus, the Son of God, until we are finally with Him. And with Him we will never grow weary or tired.

Let Us Pray:

My Father, Thank You for preparing the way for me. Thank You for getting my room ready for when this journey has been finished. You are with me the entire time, and You have promised that You will always be there with me, even when I turn the wrong way and take my eyes off of You. I praise You now and always.

One final thought

I know that some people that may have read this entire book still may not have taken that first step and asked for forgiveness and mercy from God. Let me assure you that God does love you, He will never leave you, and He is ready to accept You as His own. All you need to do is ask:

> "God, I am a sinner, and I am not worthy to come before You. But I have heard that You sent Your Son, Jesus, to be the sacrifice for my sin. You sent Your Son to die on the cross because of the sin I have committed. Please forgive me God, please forgive my sins, and allow me to enter into Your kingdom. I know I do not deserve this; Your word tells me that no one is righteous and worthy, but

it also says You loved me so much that You took care of it by sending Your Son, Jesus to save me. For this, I thank You, for this I am eternally grateful, and I praise You for forgiving me."